Battling Floods

A Guide to Survival and Aid

I0435651

Prepping and Survival Series

M. Usman

Mendon Cottage Books

JD-Biz Publishing

Disclaimer

The information is this book is provided for informational purposes only. It is not intended to be used and medical advice or a substitute for proper medical treatment by a qualified health care provider. The information is believed to be accurate as presented based on research by the author.

The contents have not been evaluated by the U.S. Food and Drug Administration or any other Government or Health Organization and the contents in this book are not to be used to treat cure or prevent disease.

The author or publisher is not responsible for the use or safety of any diet, procedure or treatment mentioned in this book. The author or publisher is not responsible for errors or omissions that may exist.

Warning

The Book is for informational purposes only and before taking on any diet, treatment or medical procedure, it is recommended to consult with your primary health care provider.

Our books are available at

1. Amazon.com
2. Barnes and Noble
3. Itunes
4. Kobo
5. Smashwords
6. Google Play Books

Table of Contents

Preface

Floods are the rage of nature brought about by the combination of its wrath and human negligence. We will try to explain the techniques and tips for flood survival, in this book.

We start off by explaining the different kinds of floods, what causes them, and how human actions have increased the level of flood intensity over time. Awareness is a strong weapon and one of the most useful ones in combating any natural calamity. We explain the associated risks with your various locations and give you advice in coping with different scenarios.

Section three leads you through every tool necessary for battling and defending these scenarios. Coping with disaster without first aid and helping materials is a catastrophic situation. Lastly, we guide you further in matters of what to do after a flood and finish off with the first aid techniques for the most common injuries that you might have the misfortune to face.

Chapter 1 – Introduction

One of the most common occurring and havoc creating disasters known to mankind are floods. Not only does it cost every nation billions of dollars in economic losses, but it is also deadly in human sufferings. According to research extending from the period of 1988 to 1997, floods cost the American, on average, $3.7 billion annually, and moreover, the loss in human lives was around 110 annually. This monstrous damage is as bad as almost all the rest of the natural calamities combined. When it waves around you, escaping its wrath is a task not to be taken lightly.

Now the question that arises in your mind is certainly; "What on earth causes such a disaster anyway and can't we do something about it?"

Well, floods occur in specific known locations called floodplains. These areas typically receive a prolonged rainfall or several short bursts of showers in a smaller span. Any kind of ice or debris collapse can also become a target against all your weapons for the survival of floods. The deadly combination of the melting of snow and the thunders of rain can create havoc if they burst out of the human barriers set to restrain them.

Now the more dangerous kinds of floods are called flash floods. What sets them apart and makes them more deadly is the short period in which they can occur. Flash floods don't give you much of a warning beforehand and there are no set systems that can really prevent and control them in a set spare time. So if you get caught in a flash flood unprepared, that can be disastrous. Luckily flash floods can only strike certain areas. These floods can occur due to a heavy rainfall event, damage in the dam, or breaking of a levee. Since the damage is restricted to people in all these areas, they have to prepare themselves at all times to save the essentials and protect them at a moment's notice.

All this urbanization has increased the effectiveness of the damage created by a flood. In a natural terrain the land has the ability to absorb the water from the heavy rainfall. The building of roads and infrastructure takes away this ability from the land and streets become rivers and the lower floors, and especially the basements, become fatal ground as the water fills them up in seconds.

So, all in all we saw that the factors that might assist and contribute to floods are the intensity and time period of the rain fall. These two are the key. Obviously other factors, like terrain, that we just discussed also impact, but they are more focused on reducing or enhancing the damage created.

Chapter 2 - Awareness Information

Awareness is the key and your best chances of survival. As we will learn, especially in the case of flash floods, time is not your friend and losing a moment can be your last big mistake. Your area will have a local emergency management office to call about the scenarios explained above and ask them for information and plan accordingly. National weather service and the American Red Cross are a few examples and may vary with the area or zone in which you are located.

Differentiating Warnings and Watches

Now, it is very important to act timely in a disaster situation. The awareness comes through the media, but it is important that we filter out the information accurately. Wrong interpretation of any news is going to be really harmful for you.

- A watch is a message transmitted by the National weather service about the possibility of an approaching thunderstorm over the next six hours, covering certain areas. This is no different than the everyday weather reports about sunny or snowy approaching conditions. Every local office covers a certain territory and gives awareness information. Keep in mind that this is information way in advance of any disaster occurring.

- A warning, on the other hand, sounds more immediate doesn't it? It is in fact the shortest possibly notice that can be handed out to you, possibly issued when a disaster is as soon as thirty minutes away from you. It is released on a county by county basis.

A watch, therefore, is the first sign of approaching danger; get ready when you get this. If you stay lax and wait for a warning you might be in potentially big trouble.

Be Aware of Flood Hazards

Floods have the capability to be immensely disastrous and we implore that you do not take them lightly by any means. A flood in flow can tear out the trees from their very roots and move boulders into your path, not to mention, the load of debris that it carries with it. All of these add to the power of a flood apart from its natural power, which is the rushing water itself. Floods can reach up to alarming heights of twenty feet above the ground.

When caught in a flood, there is simply no time to think or innovate. You have to keep the mantra very simple and that simplicity is to immediately head to higher ground and keep a decent distance from the flood waters. Do not be fooled by any shallow depths. The force a fast flowing flood can create is too big for you to fight. The foolish things that you have to avoid are basically trying to walk, swim, or drive in the scenario of a flood. Even two feet of flood waters are enough to overpower your vehicle and make it a part of the flood debris.

Plan for a Flood

- We say it again and again and seriously we cannot insist with more intensity, but planning beforehand is the key. You have to cover all essential information and to start off, you have to understand the locality where you reside and the flood risk it has according to its elevation.

- In conditions predicting a flood, contact the nearest Red Cross, the local national weather service office, or any other planning department in your zone for assistance.

If you are at risk from floods:

- If your area is prone to floods make sure that you get in touch with your insurance agent. It is an excellent idea to back up to all your losses.

- Keep a battery powered radio; you have to remain in touch with the outside world at all times for any updates and emergency messages.

If your house is in a flood zone

- It is ironic that you may end up searching for water to drink as it overflows your entire house. However, you cannot drink contaminated water and need to ensure that, before the situation worsens, you keep a sufficient amount of water stored for your family. Sinks, bathtubs and all bottles can act as reservoirs in this situation.

- Keep in mind that all unsecured items will become a part of the flood. Bring outdoor belongings inside to be washed off, and stored inside.

- Higher floors are naturally safer, so move all your most valuable items to the top floor of your house.

- You may be advised by the local authorities to turn off the utility supplies. This is good advice and you should act on it to avoid any further catastrophe.

- It is this moment that your disaster kit will be coming in handy. We shall explain the contents of the kit in the next section.

- At the first watch sign, make sure that your car is fueled up. Believe me you do not want to have a car half filled when you are on the run for your precious life.

- Evacuate at a moment's notice.

Instructions to Children

- Be alert and alarmed. Upon encounter with floods, immediately change your direction and turn towards higher ground. Water, even as low as six inches deep, can sweep you off your feet and believe me it's not a charming prospect.

- Flooded areas that give the indication of stillness in the water are still dangerous and their levels may yet rise again, so keep yourself at a distance from them.

- I know children are intrigued by the prospect of gathered water, but you have to make them believe that it is dangerous and not a pond. The debris may cut them at several places and walking or swimming can give them injuries or even be deadly for them.

- Do not stay in your vehicles. They can be swept away with the flood, so immediately get out safely and move to higher ground.

- One of the leading causes of death in floods is from snake bites. Watch out for these venomous creatures. The speed of the floods carries these snakes out from their homes and closer to their prey.

- The banks of recently flooded areas are an extremely unstable region to be in. They can give way to the moving water without a moment's notice.

- Do not eat anything that has come into contact with the flood water as they are now certainly contaminated with all sorts of germs and bacteria. Sickness is unavoidable if you eat even a tiny part of it.

How to Protect Your Property

- During the emergency and the panic, it will be next to impossible to gather all your essential documentations and store them away safely. In all that rush you will not even be able to locate or recall half of the important stuff. So, before the disaster, keep your valuable documents IDs, insurance papers etc. in a safe box and store it away on a higher ground.

- Now some communities absolutely say no to any kind of building in the known floodplains. If you are taking this risk make sure that you elevate your structure properly and take all the necessary precautions.

- All water heaters and electric panels should be placed on higher floors. An unharmed water heater can be a good source of clean water supply in this disaster situation.

- It is important that you prevent the flood water from entering into your drainage systems too. For this precaution, use check valves while building the sewer traps. You can also use large stoppers in your basins and tubs.

- While residing in areas that are prone to floods, make sure that you build some barriers to protect your place from the floods. You may need authorization, but you can easily get that from the local authorities. Flood walls and levees can be designed beautifully to serve this purpose.

- Seepage through cracks and damaged areas can be a pain in the neck, so seal the walls in your basements especially, and make them waterproof to avoid this scenario.

- You local emergency management office will have a contingency plan and may be able to provide you with certain guidance to mitigate any further damage. These resources might be particular to your areas so leave no stone unturned to protect yourself.

Chapter 3 - Assemble a Disaster Supplies Kit

It is very important that you have a disaster supply kit prepared and ready before the unforeseen damaging event takes place. This is especially meant for people whose areas suffer from floods regularly. Assembling these items is only advantageous to you if they are done beforehand. This section will help you in dealing with all possible items that you need to check in your all important list. It is absolutely crucial that you include your children in all discussions of the evacuation plans. All marked supply locations should also be known to them and a drill should be carried out to ensure their participation.

Prepare Your Kit

Important Tips

- You may not always be at home when the disaster strikes, and in that case, all your efforts will become futile if the emergency supplies are at home. To avoid this from happening, keep a smaller kit of these supplies in your car. This will sustain you for a while.

- All items should be in air tight plastic bags; in the case of floods this is very important as all the items have to be protected from damages.

- All the food and water supplies have to be refreshed every six months to keep them fresh.

- Your prescription medications have to be stocked up; use the advice of your pharmacist in storing all these drugs as their temperatures and surroundings affect the drugs.

Disaster Supplies Kit Basics

The items listed below should be kept in a safe location known to all family members. The location should be easily accessible in the times of a natural disaster.

- Signal flare.

- A portable, battery-powered radio

- Extra batteries

- Supply of prescription medications

- First aid kit

- Personal identification

- Flashlight

- Matches in a waterproof container

- Credit card

- Cash

- An extra set of car keys

- Map of the area

Evacuation Supplies Kit

An important thing to be kept in mind is that all the containers should be labeled carefully; this will help you from getting into any panicky situations while the disaster strikes.

Disaster Supplies Kit basics

- For each person, keep at least three gallons of water.

- A three day supply, at minimum, for the food items that are non perishable.

- Kitchen accessories: these include paper cups, plates, disposable utensils, knives, and basic cooking items like sugar salt and various spices.

- A strong pair of shoes for each member and a single change of clothes are also good to be kept at your side. Raingear and thermal wears can be a good idea as well.

- Blankets

- Sleeping bags

- Important tools and accessories: It's important to carry accessories like pencil, paper, and even threads and needles. Small canisters to store stuff, plastic sheeting, and compasses etc.

- Sanitation and hygiene items: These include toilet papers, towels, toothbrushes and pastes, disinfectants and a small shovel.

- Books, they'll be your companion to kill time.

To Build a Makeshift Toilet

Stranded outside your house has several major and minor issues, one such issue is finding a makeshift toilet. Use a garbage bag and line it up around a bucket. Place two boards on them to make a usable seat. Use a disinfectant after every use to ensure cleanliness. When not in use, also make a habit of covering the bucket tightly. Bury your waste; this will help in avoiding any attracted rats and insects.

First Aid Kit

The following are some of the most basic first aid items that you may require:

- Sterile adhesive bandages

- First aid manual

- Sunscreen

- Needle

- Safety pins

- Cleansing soap

- Latex gloves

- Tweezers

- Triangular bandages

- Non-prescription drugs

- Scissors

- Antiseptic

- Moistened towels

- Thermometer

- Tube of petroleum jelly

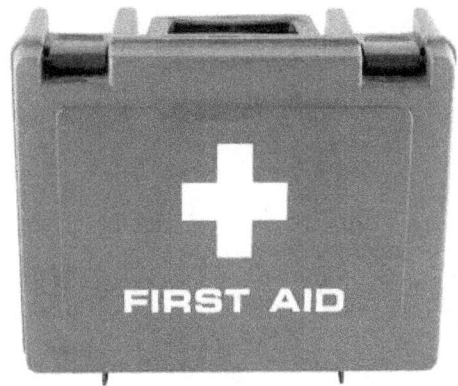

Have the following non-prescription drugs in your Disaster Supplies Kit:

- Antacid

- Aspirin

- Anti diarrheal medication

- Laxative

- Anti-allergy medicines

- Anti-emetics

- Common cold and fever relievers

Important Documents

All the following documents are your essential keys of recognition of various important uses in this world. Keep them in a safe box beforehand and make a list of all the important pieces of documents. What these following enlist is basically only to give you an idea:

- Will

- Social security cards

- Bank account numbers

- Insurance policies

- Immunization records

- Contracts

- Family records (birth, marriage, death certificates)

- Stocks and bonds

- Passports

- Credit card account numbers

- Inventory of valuable household goods

- Important telephone number

No matter how random things appear, one should always have a plan. The floods do not leave you ample time to get what you need and then escape. These ruthless forces of nature will wipe away your chances of survival with the delay of minor seconds. Gather all items beforehand and ensure their rechecking and safe collection as soon as the watch has been given out. Always prepare for the worst and pray that the damage has finally turned out to be on the minimum side. We are hereby providing you with some important stuff to be prepared beforehand.

Water

Drinking water will become an issue as the contaminated flood water is not a choice to be drank. Apart from that, your current supplies may get damaged or contaminated by the floods. You will need a hydrated body to survive the two or three grueling days that may follow. You need to make sure that your water supply lasts for at least three days. Fill the tubs and containers in the top floors of the house. You may also freeze water in plastic containers.

Sanitation

The very air is infected and feels uneasy during the incidence of a flood. In these circumstances keeping yourself clean and maintaining good hygiene can be great for your health. The long term benefits of keeping sanitation kits with you will be great and the following are certain must items that you should have:

- Bleach

- Toilet paper

- Soap

- Hand wipes

- Person hygiene items

- Feminine hygiene items

Disaster Tools

Time will be short and decision making might be easy, but carrying out certain decisions for practicality might require tools. The following is a set of tools that can act as a life saver:

- Batteries

- Battery operated radio

- Multipurpose tools
- Propane stove
- Duct tape
- Fire extinguisher
- Waterproof matches
- Floatation device
- Can opener
- Tube tent
- Pliers
- Plastic cups and plates
- Trash bags
- Signal flare
- Whistle
- Wrench to shut off gas
- Compass

Chapter 4 - What to do Before Flooding Occurs

- When you can observe that you are experiencing continuous showers and live in an area that has a history of floods, be aware because this is the first sign.

- Immediately take out your battery powered radio and keep it tuned to the local radio channel for any updates or tragic news.

- Make sure if you are driving and plan to stop, to allow the showers to ease up and do not park the car in the vicinity of any kind of a stream. A dam can break and make the stream overflow in matter of seconds.

What to do During a Flood WATCH

The following are the steps to be ensured as soon as a flood watch has been issued:

- Be in touch with the outside world. Using a battery operated radio has its advantages, because in the events of any natural disaster, the electricity supplies may discontinue for a while. Use this radio to tune in to your local channels to find out your particular situation.

- This is the best time to implement all the disaster instructions and give final touches and checking to your first aid supply bags.

- Do not hesitate and in the extreme cases be ready to evacuate at a moment's notice. Nothing is more precious than the lives of your family.

What to Do During a Flood WARNING

The following steps are to be followed as soon as a flood warning has been issued:

- Warnings are much more serious and panic worthy situations. Firstly, a warning issued by your local authorities' means that there is not much time and you have to take all the precautions in a very limited time now.

- As we repeated earlier as well, saving lives is the key. In case of extreme emergencies, forget about everything and if you live in a flood-prone area move to higher ground. The only thing that should be in your mind is the safety of your family and friends.

- The advice of the local authorities has to be followed at all times. There should be no exception and this point cannot be stressed with greater importance. They will recommend you safe routes; taking shortcuts that are not recommended may not be a wise idea as they might be blocked.

- Timely withdrawing from the scene of flood is the best idea.

What to do if You Are Driving During a Flood

- If you are stuck in this tragedy while driving on the road you have to make certain quick witted decisions. You have to avoid the already flooded routes. Most causalities occurs when people become reckless and underestimate the floods by driving through the streams, and some actually even playing in them. There is always a possibility of the roadbed being washed out by the floods causing you to become trapped. The rising water can damage the engine thus seizing your car and forcing it to go away in the flood.

- Avoid all roads and routes that are on a lower level and always seek to go higher up the altitude scale to avoid floods.

- In the scenario where you get trapped in the water and your engine gives away, DO NOT try to move in the stalled vehicle. Too many deaths have happened due to this faulty decision making. The force that the rushing waters exert on your vehicle is around 500 pounds and you simply cannot hope to beat it. On average, one foot of travelling water displaces approximately 1500 pounds of the weight of the car, therefore it is possible to assume that two feet of water can displace the entire weight of an average vehicle. So, the best thing you can do is to immediately leave the vehicle to ensure your safety.

What to do After a Flood or Flash Flood

- You ought to be thanking your Lord if you got away with minor injuries only. Immediately get them sorted out from the nearby medical centers, and more detail will be given about this in the next section.

- If you find yourself safe and free from the consequences of the floods, seek people that may require your help and starting from neighbors is the best way to go. This multiplicative affect of helping everyone out is the essence of a community.

- Do not seek shelter in any building that is surrounded by floods. What may happen is that the flood water can overcome the foundations of any building and weaken the base, and the floors can start breaking and cracking. In the worst case scenario the building might even collapse.

- Also, do not seek shelter in buildingsa that are not yet cleared by the local authorities, as there might be incidences of gas leakages inside the premises and that can be fatal.

When you see that the signs of the premises are clear, then enter the building while taking the following precautions:

- Wear strong shoes to combat the debris.

- Flashlights are the ideal object to carry around with you as they will enable you to examine the building without the likelihood of you setting the place on fire due to any gas leakages.

- Do take a round to examine the walls, windows, and staircases to make sure that the buildings pose no sudden danger.

- Gas leakages are a nightmare in any disaster situation. It is the worst disaster aftermath possible. The slightest of sparks can bring about a colossal explosion. Any hissing sound should catch your attention and if that happens, simply open the window and evacuate the building turning the main gas valve off from outside the building. The gas authorities should be notified as the valve should only be opened by a professional once it has been turned off.

- Use a strong piece of wood to poke through the flood or the debris to watch out for loose floorings and, most importantly, any lurking animals. Snakes especially become a participant in the wrecking of a flood.

After returning home:

- Throw away any food items that have accidently come into any amount of contact with the flood water. The food item gets immediately contaminated and can be really harmful. Any canned item that has been damaged or dented should not be used as well, as these infections spread very rapidly.

- Drinking water has to be handled with care as well and any water that has a questionable smell or feeling should be boiled and distilled before drinking. Drinking contaminated water can be drastic for your heath, therefore you should immediately call local authorities to check the water supplies in your house.

- Do not pump out the water that has flooded your basements immediately and go through this process gradually. If you do it all at once the soil outside your house would become water saturated and might cause your foundations to weaken.

- Service the damaged pits, pools, and septic tanks to get them cleansed as soon as possible.

- Take pictures of all the incurred damages to face the insurance claims.

Chapter 5 - Treating flood injuries

Floods bring about quite a variety of injuries, from the cuts and bruises by the debris to venomous snake bites. In this section, we will help you in seeking out certain first aid tips that will make your heath better.

First aid tips:

The first and foremost necessity, is to clean your hands and not only clean them but purify them with soap and water that is fit to be drank.

Bleeding

Let us firstly turn our attention to the result of the cutting edge sharp debris that flows with the floods. Below are some tips for dealing with bleeding injuries:

❖　　Act instantly

❖　　Use gloves

❖　　Bleeding makes the patient dizzy, make him lie down

❖　　Apply pressure to the wounded area

❖　　Raise and reduce the movement of the wounded part

❖　　Cover up the wound and apply a bandage

❖　　Do not use cotton wool for treatment as they complicate the wound

❖　　Call emergency services for severe cases

Lacerations and Cuts

Cuts are similar to bleeding wounds, but they differ in the amount of damage done to the area by the flowing debris. Follow the instructions below to tend to them:

- ❖ Wear strong boots

- ❖ Use gloves

- ❖ Clean the cut with saline or boiled water that has been cooled

- ❖ Use non adherent bandage/ dressing cut from being exposed to flood water as that might attract an infection.

- ❖ If exposed, use sterile dressing after carefully washing the cut with soap.

- ❖ Seek medical attention if color changes or swelling starts.

Sprains and strains

There is a very simple formula for remembering the first aid provision to sprains. It is termed RICE management, where each alphabet letter corresponds to the treatment to be ensured.

- ❖ R – Rest the injured part of the patient.

- ❖ I – Ice packs should be wrapped in a cloth and applied to the injured part for fifteen minutes. The process should be repeated every two hours for the first day. If ice is not available, you can make use of cold water too.

- ❖ C – Compression bandages have been applied in a way that they should extend from the injurious part.

- ❖ E – Elevate the part that has suffered the damage.

Snake bites

These unforgiving creatures create a lot of torment in the incidence of a flood. Follow the steps cautiously and seek medical attention as well.

❖ Avoid deep waters.

❖ Wear really thick boots.

❖ Make sure that the smallest possible amount of your skin is bare.

❖ Try to remember the color and shape of the bite, as that can be helpful in seeking the anti venom.

❖ Do not wash the skin around the bite.

❖ Make the patient relax and lie down.

❖ Apply an immobilization bandage from the tips of the fingers or toes to the stretch of the limb and apply pressure.

❖ Immobilize the limb with the help of a splint. Check circulation in fingers or toes (check blood supply in fingers or toes; see below)

❖ To check if the blood supply is restricted or not press the fingernail or toenails to see if it turns white and the color returns within 2 seconds. If the test is successful then the supply is unrestricted.

Conclusion

All in all, we request that you be prepared for the worst and hope for the best. As you could see through the entire context, our aim has been to make you realise the gravity of the situation. Floods really give you very little time to make peace with your demons and thinking calmly might become impossible.

Follow our instructions diligently and pack your bags beforehand, especially if you live in an area that is prone to floods. Life is short and is more precious than any worldly possessions, so we request that you not hesitate, even for a moment, in leaving the house behind for you and your family's safety.

Author Bio

Muhammad Usman is a distinguished medical graduate of Allama Iqbal medical college (AIMC). He is a professional writer who has been in the field for more than 4 years. During this time he has produced 10,000+ articles, blogs and eBooks on various niches related to diseases, health, fitness, nutrition and well-being. He is a regular contributor to several journals related to medicine and surgery. He is the editor of several journals and newspapers.

Check out some of the other JD-Biz Publishing books

Gardening Series on Amazon

Health Learning Series

Country Life Books

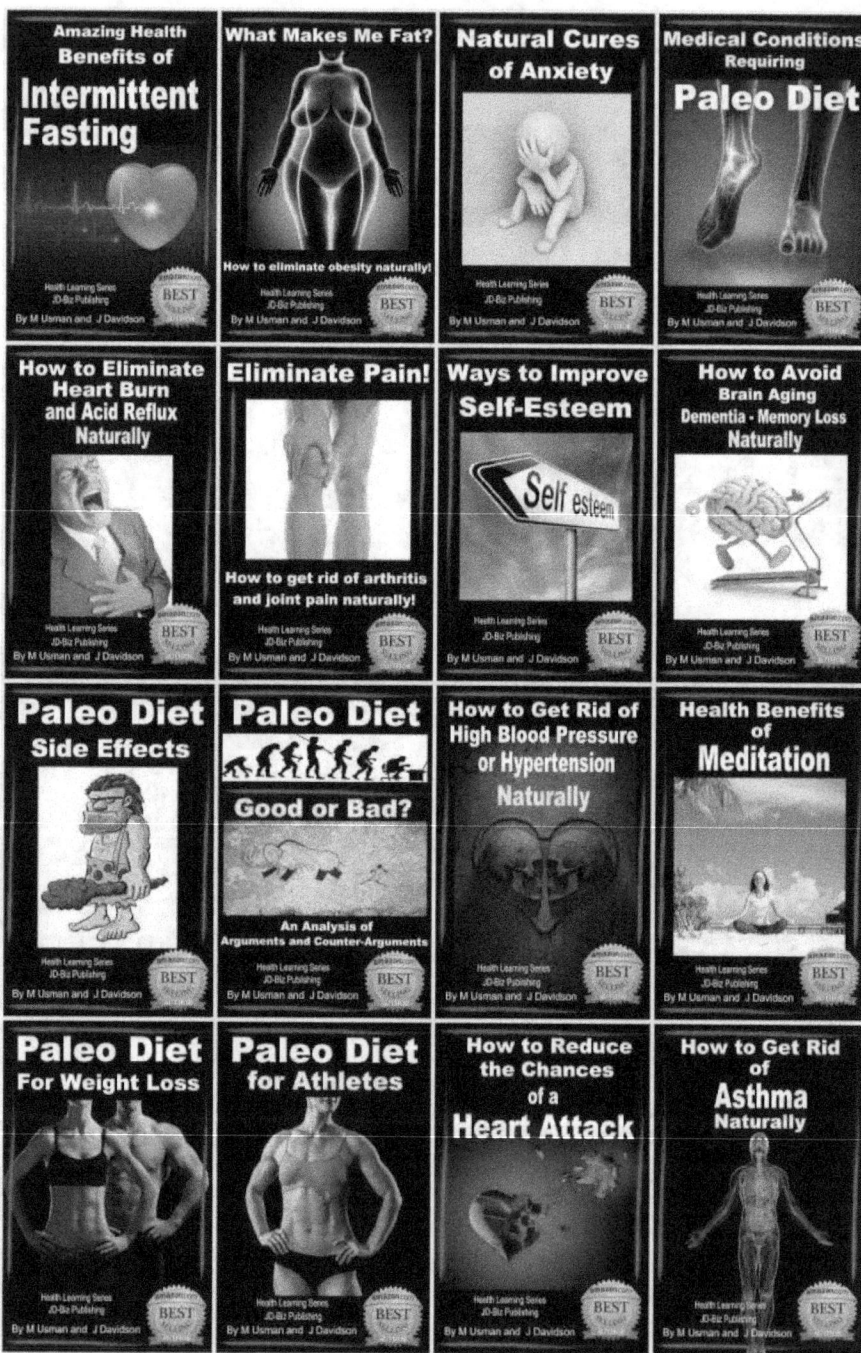

Amazing Animal Book Series

Learn To Draw Series

How to Build and Plan Books

Entrepreneur Book Series

Our books are available at

1. Amazon.com

2. Barnes and Noble

3. Itunes

4. Kobo

5. Smashwords

6. Google Play Books

Publisher

JD-Biz Corp

P O Box 374

Mendon, Utah 84325

http://www.jd-biz.com/

www.ingramcontent.com/pod-product-compliance
Lightning Source LLC
Chambersburg PA
CBHW071152280526
45787CB00003B/1494